Nintendo Strategic Analysis Paper

Jessica Phillips

Bibliographic information published by the German National Library:

The German National Library lists this publication in the National Bibliography; detailed bibliographic data are available on the Internet at http://dnb.dnb.de.

ISBN: 9783346295651
This book is also available as an ebook.

Print and binding: Books on Demand GmbH, Norderstedt, Germany
Printed on acid-free paper from responsible sources.

The present work has been carefully prepared. Nevertheless, authors and publishers do not incur liability for the correctness of information, notes, links and advice as well as any printing errors.

GRIN web shop: https://www.grin.com/document/955573

NINTENDO CORPORATION STRATEGIC ANALYSIS

Jessica Phillips-
October 7, 2020

A thorough examination of Nintendo Corporation's business strategies.

Contents

Introduction

Nintendo Corporation was established on September 23rd of 1889 by Fusajiro Yamauchi in Kyoto Japan. The company originally sold hand painted Hanafuda playing cards under the name Nintendo Koppai. Their success in the playing card industry led to them to try other ventures such as ramen noodles, taxi services, short-term "love" hotels and lastly video games. In 1940 Fusajiro Yamauchi died and nine years later his great grandson Hiroshi Yamauchi took over the company at the age of 22. For the next 50 years he led Nintendo to become the video game giant it is. In 1985 Nintendo released the Nintendo Entertainment System (NES) their first home console. In 1989 they released the Gameboy their first handheld device. Though neither item was the first of its kind they still were wildly popular and pushed Nintendo to create newer and better games and consoles. (Gebel, 2019)

Nintendo's Mission and Vision statement today is lacking. The company is known for their creativity and innovation, but their mission statement is void of that.

"Nintendo of America's Corporate Mission and Philosophy: At Nintendo we are proud to be working for the leading company in our industry. We are strongly committed to producing and marketing the best products and support services available. We believe it is essential not only to provide products of the highest quality, but to treat every customer with attention, consideration, and respect. By listening closely to our customers, we constantly improve our products and services. We feel an equal commitment toward our employees. We want to maintain an atmosphere in which talented individuals can work together as a team. Commitment and enthusiasm are crucial to the high quality of our products and support services. We believe in treating our employees with the same consideration and respect that we, as a company, show our customers." (Nintendo, 2020)

Nintendo's long and short-term issues in the organization stem from their competition and their need to keep and acquire new customers. Compared to its rivals, Nintendo is the most innovative. Which gives them an edge when it comes to attracting and reaching a new customer base. This is a long-term issue for them however, this requires them to continually create new games, accessories, and or consoles to pique the interest of new and old customers alike. It takes work to keep them coming back for more. Their short-term issue is their competition releasing a new console or other large new additions to their competitions. This is a short-term issue because every five years or so Nintendo's rivals release new systems. Meaning when the new systems release a new set of short-term issues arise and the earlier ones drop away. Though Nintendo does not truly compete with it is rivals in the sense of releasing a system before its competition that technology wise is better, faster, and quieter. It does things on its own terms. They create a new console and release it and though technology wise it may not be better than their competitors it is great in its own way. The primary example of this is that the Switch is not just a standard console that plugs into your television, it is also a handheld device that allows for seamless transition between its two functions. Neither of Nintendo's rivals can do this at all, or anything like it. (Gamble, 2008)

Environment

Internal

Nintendo's marketing strategy is to sell high quality family friendly consoles, games, and accessories at an affordable price. The company continually works on innovative solutions that add value for the customers, while reducing costs of the consoles. The company effectively uses their suppliers, employees, and financing to help reduce costs that they pass on to their customers. Nintendo Corporation prides themselves on listening to their customers and supplying a product that the customer wants. (Nintendo, 2020)

The competitive advantage that Nintendo holds over its rivals is their intellectual property. The make more of a profit creating and selling their own games than if they were to use third party developers. If they used third party developers than Nintendo would make very minimal off of game sales (10 15%) instead of making 100% of the profits. (Farhoomand, 2008) They have an extreme brand loyalty with their customers because of that intellectual property. Nintendo does not sell off their characters or games to other companies, which means for their customers they must go to Nintendo to play more. Keeping their intellectual property limits the sales they could make on some of their popular games. However, it leads to more sales for Nintendo just so the customer can play a game. An example of this would be that you really want to play the new Smash Brothers game but you do not own a Switch, the only way you will get to play Smash Brothers would be to purchase a Switch. Because of their customers extreme brand

4

loyalty, they are willing to pay for the system to get to play the new game. In 2006 I personally proved that brand loyalty can be an extremely effective way to get customers to buy your products for life. Nintendo instilled in me a love for their Zelda games. I have been playing them since the NES. I love Zelda so much I even have a tattoo from it. In 2006 I camped out and bought the Wii when it was first released. I had no interest in any other thing the Wii offered I only wanted to play the Zelda game. That brand loyalty they built in me by creating a character and immersive worlds got me to camp out in front of a Best Buy for 19 hours. After the 19 hours we were let into the store where I proceeded to spend around $400 on a Wii and everything, I would need to play the new Zelda game. (Kain, 2020)

When looking at the sales of consoles in the current console war PlayStation holds the competitive advantage with its PS4 sales at 112.3 million, The Switch 61.44 million, and Xbox One has only 41 million. (Sirani, 2020) Microsoft is trailing on console sale but they have a heavy online presence with 90 million subscribers (Summers, 2020), Sony has 38.8 million subscribers (Lyerly, 2020) and Nintendo has 15 million. (Doolan, 2020) PlayStation offers 5,015 games currently, Nintendo has 4,530 games, and the Xbox One has a measly 1,938 games available to play. The one place that Nintendo has a lead is the total number of consoles and handheld devices sold. They have sold a cumulative amount of 772.4 million units, Sony has sold 555.69 million units, and lastly Microsoft has sold 160 million units. (Nintendo, 2020)

To examine the external environment of Nintendo we need to look at the opportunities and threats the company has. Michael E. Porter Created a framework which uses "five forces that shape competition within an industry: (1) the risk of entry by potential competitors, (2) the intensity of rivalry among established companies within an industry, (3) the bargaining power of buyers, (4) the bargaining power of suppliers, (5) the closeness of substitutes to an industry product" (Hill Charles W. L., 2020)(page 43 line 36).

New companies are entering the video game industry daily which is a greater risk and threat for Nintendo to gain more competition. Large companies like Google are introducing new platforms (Stadia) which require no console, no downloads, and no updates to play any game available. (Google, 2020)

When it comes to the intensity of rivalry in the video game industry it is extraordinarily strong. Both PlayStation and Microsoft are fiercely competitive. Both try to beat each other by having the best technology and earliest release date. Which is fine and dandy for them, but Nintendo does things on their own terms. They do feel the heat from their competitors, they just reacted differently. Instead of beating them at their own game Nintendo by passed them and created their own product that made them unique. They chose to go down a path that their competitors did not take making this an opportunity for them. (Gamble, 2008)

Nintendo uses the bargaining power of its buyers by supplying them something they can not get anywhere else. Their products can only be played and used with other Nintendo products. Their characters and video games do not cross over onto any systems. The brand loyalty of Nintendo's customers is a positive aspect for them. Nintendo goes above and beyond to listen to their customers and incorporate changes that will please them. They want to make every experience a great one. Parents know that they can purchase any Nintendo product and it will be age appropriate for all the members of the household. The bargaining power of its buyers is an opportunity for Nintendo. (Nintendo, 2020)

The bargaining power of Nintendo's suppliers is a risk to them. Nintendo strives to supply a product that is top quality and still affordable. If their suppliers were to raise their cost to high, then Nintendo would be forced to either raise prices or go with an inferior product. However, the market is flooded with suppliers that can guarantee the same product at a better price. There becomes a battle to be the supplier for Nintendo and that the bargaining power of the supplier turns into an opportunity for Nintendo because the suppliers are offering the same products at different values. Which allows Nintendo to pick the best priced product and pass those savings along. (Sun, 2017)

The last item Porter speaks about is the threat from substitute products on the market. There are several products on the market that you can play video games on (PlayStation 4, XBOX One, computers, and even phones) but none are quite like the Switch. A gaming laptop would be the closest, in that you can connect it to a tv and play that way or take the computer to go and play. However, you need a laptop that is not a basic stock laptop to play and those cost drastically more than The Switch. Because the Switch is so unique compared to what is on the market there are not really substitutes for it and that is an opportunity for Nintendo. The have completely taken control of this part of the market. There is also no other company that offers the games that Nintendo makes. If you want to play your favorite Nintendo character games than you must play them on a Nintendo product.

Strategies

There are many strategies a business can follow to position itself into the optimal spot in the marketplace that will support the best competitive advantages. A standard strategy is implemented when a company makes a basic product meant for the average consumer. A broad low-cost strategy sells to the entire market but at the lowest cost. A broad differentiation strategy sells to the standard consumer, but they offer different products for different segments. An example of this would be a company that makes toothpaste. They make toothpaste that can be used by anyone, but they also offer toothpaste designated for children, or sensitive teeth, and or whitening. The next two strategies are focused ones. Which means they do not make products for everyone; they make products for particular segments of the market. The focus low-cost strategy makes products for a several market segments and or just one at the lowest cost available on the market. The focus differentiation strategy involves making different products for several segments in the market but not the entire market. An example of this would be a company that makes prescription eyeglasses. They make different glasses for all the segments it sells too. A segmentation strategy as well sells different products to each segment except they sell to the entire market not just a few segments. Lastly the Blue Ocean Strategy is when a company completely reinvents a product and makes it different than any other product like it and in a sense create a new market for themselves. (Hill Charles W. L., 2020)

In the past Nintendo has used a Blue Ocean Strategy to disrupt the marketplace. Their Game Cube console was not a big hit, they sold only 22 million. It was their lowest selling product. Nintendo needed a real winner to continue to compete in the video game home console marketplace. However, Nintendo had no footing when it came to competing head to head with their rivals so they decided to shake the whole market up by releasing a product that no-one else was working on. To quote Satoru Iwata, the President of Nintendo CO. Ltd. "For some time, we have believed the game industry is ready for disruption. Not just from Nintendo, but from all game developers. It is what we all need to expand our audience. It is what we need to expand our imaginations." (Iwata, 2006) The Nintendo Wii saved Nintendo from financial ruin. They sold 105 million units of the Wii. The Blue Ocean Strategy is not the only strategy Nintendo employees, they also use a focus differentiation and standard strategy. Though video games are not played by everyone (the entire market) Nintendo still tries to make a product that anyone can pick up and play. They make their games simple to understand, play, and are appropriate for all ages. They strive to make a family friendly product that the entire family will want to play together. Design a product that is a standard item that anyone and everyone can use even though not everyone has interest in video games. You miss 100% of the chances you do not take and that is what Nintendo has avoided by making their product for everyone not just those who enjoy the industry. They differentiate their product for different segments by creating different types of game genres and accessories to go with them. One example of this would be making games for racing and a steering wheel controller you can use with the games. (Farhoomand, 2008)

Conclusion

To become the top company in the video game industry Nintendo would need to do some work period if they want to gain the competitive advantage in the video game industry their new console would require technology that is better than the new systems that Microsoft and Sony are releasing soon , on top of the qualities that already make it unique. They also need to release more games to surpass Sony's extensive library. They are adding their older Nintendo 64 games which will help but they will still need to add more games. The last improvement they could make would be to add more online content, a game streaming app that you can pay monthly to play would increase their profits and monthly subscriptions. As is Nintendo's differences and their intellectual property is what is keeping them popular and relevant.

References

Doolan, L. (2020, January 30). *The Switch Online Service Now Has More Than 15 Million Subscribers*. Retrieved from

    Nintendolife:

    https://www.nintendolife.com/news/2020/01/the_switch_online_service_now_has_more_than_15_million_subscrib

    ers

Farhoomand, A. (2008). *Nintendo's disruptive strategy: Implications for the video game industry*. The University of Hong Kong.

    Hong Kong: Asia Case Research Centre. Retrieved 10 7, 2020, from

    http://secure.expertsmind.com/attn_files/1660_cob-nintendos%20disruptive%20strategy.pdf

Gamble, J. E. (2008). Case 14: Competition in Video Game Consoles: Sony, Microsoft, and Nintendo Battle for Supremacy. In S.

    G. Thompson, *Crafting and Executing Strategy: Concepts and Cases, 16th Edition* (pp. 489-502). New York: McGraw-

    Hill/Irwin.

Gebel, M. (2019, September 23). *25 photos of Nintendo's 130-year rise from a playing card company to fan-favorite gaming

    giant*. Retrieved from Business Insider: https://www.businessinsider.com/history-of-nintendo-130-years-video-

    games-super-mario-zelda-2019-9

Google. (2020). *Stadia Premiere Edition*. Retrieved from Google Store: https://store.google.com/us/product/stadia

Hill Charles W. L., S. M. (2020). *Strategic Management An Intergrated Approach Theory and Class*. Boston, M.A.: Cengage

    Learning, Inc.

Iwata, S. (2006, March 23). *GDC Keynote Address*. Retrieved from Nintendo World Report:

    http://www.nintendoworldreport.com\newsArt.cfm

Kain, E. (2020, Feburary 28). *The Console War Is Over Because Sony Left Microsoft Behind From The Start*. Retrieved from

    Forbes: https://www.forbes.com/sites/erikkain/2020/02/28/theres-never-really-been-a-console-war-because-

    playstation-left-xbox-behind-from-the-start/#36ba4c8313d7

Lyerly, T. (2020, Feburary 4). *37 Percent of PS4 Owners Subscribe to PlayStation Plus*. Retrieved from Game Rant:

https://gamerant.com/ps-plus-how-many-

subscribers/#:~:text=PS%20Plus%20has%2038.8%20million,in%20February%20of%20last%20year.

Nintendo. (2020). *CSR Report 2020- Putting Smiles on the Faces of Our Consumers*. Retrieved from Nintendo:

https://www.nintendo.co.jp/csr/en/report/consumers/index.html

Nintendo. (2020, June 30). *Dedicated Video Game Sales Unit* . Retrieved from Nintendo:

https://www.nintendo.co.jp/ir/en/finance/hard_soft/

Nintendo. (2020). *Nintendo of America's Corporate Mission and Philosophy*. Retrieved from Nintendo:

https://www.nintendo.com/corp/mission.jsp

O'Gorman, P. (2008). Wii: Creating a Blue Ocean. *Palermo Business Review | Nº 2 |*, pp. 97-107. Retrieved from

https://www.palermo.edu/economicas/pdf_economicas/business_paralela/review/wii.pdf

Sirani, J. (2020, August 6). *https://www.ign.com/articles/2019/10/30/top-15-best-selling-video-game-consoles-of-all-time*.

Retrieved from IGN: https://www.ign.com/articles/2019/10/30/top-15-best-selling-video-game-consoles-of-all-time

Summers, N. (2020, April 30). *Xbox Game Pass clears 10 million subscribers*. Retrieved from engadget:

https://www.engadget.com/xbox-game-pass-10-million-subscribers-

114529988.html#:~:text=Xbox%20Live%20Gold%2C%20which%20is,Shaw%2C%20lead%20communications%20for%2

0Microsoft.

Sun, L. (2017, October 3). *5 Companies That Benefit From Nintendo Switch Sales*. Retrieved from The Motley Fool :

https://www.fool.com/investing/2017/10/03/5-companies-that-benefit-from-nintendo-switch-sale.aspx

Appendices

The figure was removed by the editors for copyright reasons.

Source: Exhibit 2: Selected Information for the Best-Selling Video Game Hardware Systems, 1972-2006. Part 2: Cases in Crafting and Executing Strategy (Gamble, 2008)(page 491)

Here are the top-ten best-selling consoles of all time:

1. PlayStation 2 — 155 million units sold
2. Nintendo DS — 154.02 million units sold
3. Game Boy / Game Boy Color — 118.69 million units sold
4. PlayStation 4 — 108.9 million units sold
5. PlayStation 1 — 102.49 million units sold
6. Wii — 101.63 million units sold
7. PlayStation 3 — 87.4 million units sold
8. Xbox 360 — 84 million units sold
9. Game Boy Advance — 81.51 million units sold
10. PlayStation Portable — between 80 and 82 million units sold

(Kain, 2020)

Figure 1: Nintendo Unit Sales (except Wii), Games and Consoles, 2003-2008

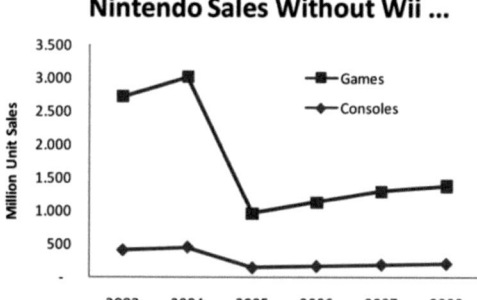

Figure 2: Nintendo Wii Unit Sales, Games and Consoles, 2003-2008

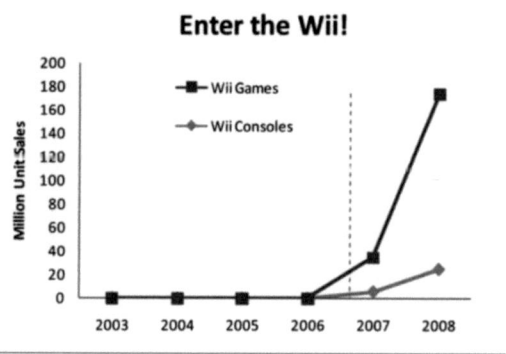

Figure 6: Cumulative Sales foe Wii, PS3 and Xbox360, March 2008-June 2008

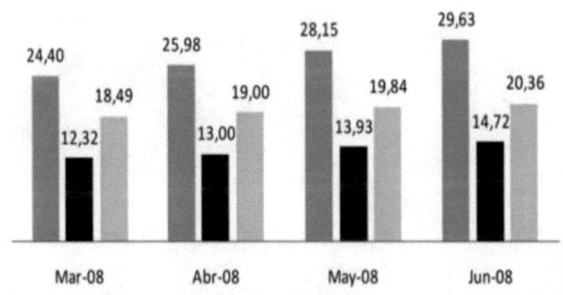

Wii leads Worldwide Sales

■ Cumulative Wii Sales ■ Cumulative PS3 Sales ▪ Cumulative Xbox360 Sales

Figure 7: Nintendo Sales Figures, 2004-2008

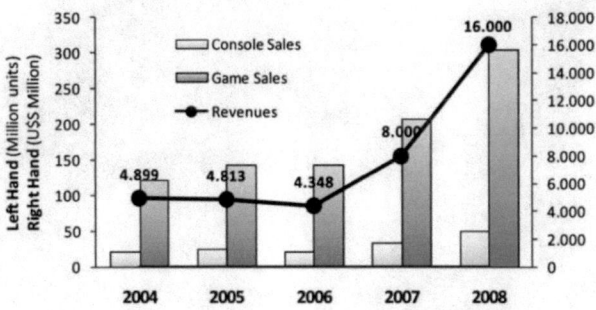

Revenue pushed by Console & Game Sales

Figure 1,2,6 & 7 (O'Gorman, 2008)

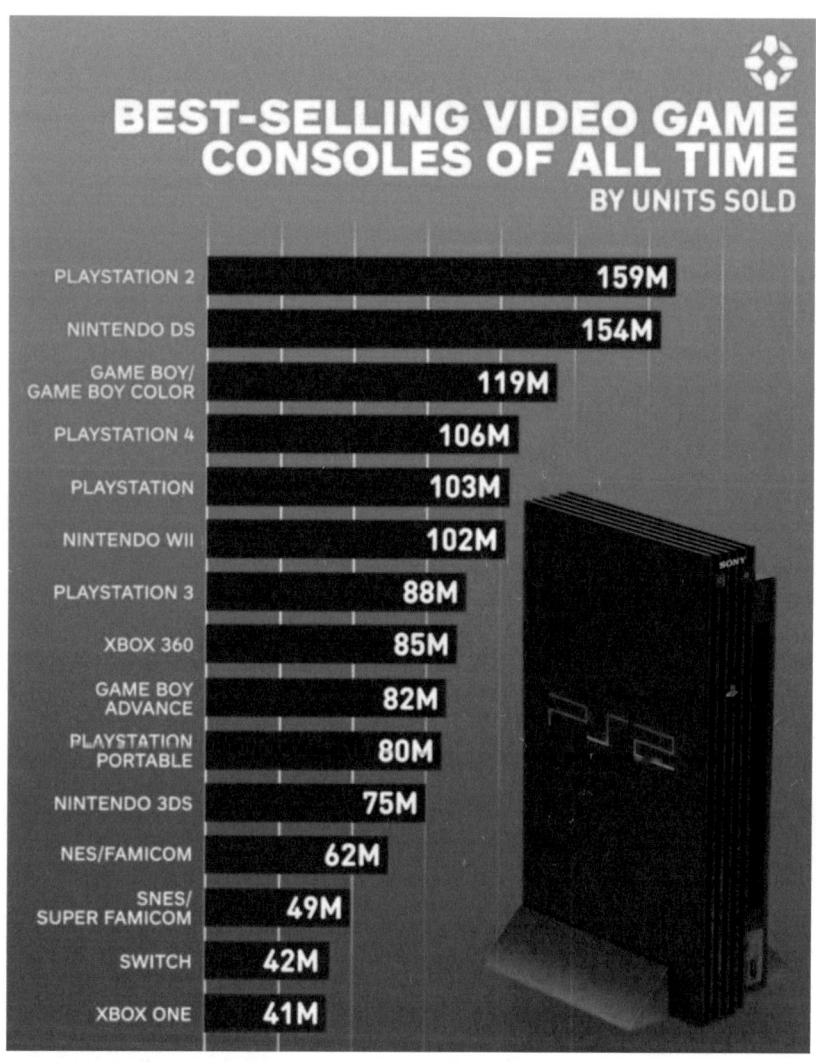

(Sirani, 2020)